BEN NIGHTHORSE CAMPBELL

NORTH AMERICAN INDIANS OF ACHIEVEMENT

BEN NIGHTHORSE CAMPBELL

Cheyenne Chief and U.S. Senator

Christopher Henry

Senior Consulting Editor

W. David Baird

Howard A. White Professor of History

Pepperdine University

CHELSEA HOUSE PUBLISHERS

New York   Philadelphia

FRONTISPIECE   Ben Nighthorse Campbell, the eighth Native American to
serve in Congress, flashes a winning smile in a 1989 photograph.

ON THE COVER   To many Americans, U.S. legislator Ben Nighthorse
Campbell epitomizes the rugged independence of the West. This portrait
shows him wearing his trademark neckerchief; the clasp is one of his
own designs.

Chelsea House Publishers
EDITORIAL DIRECTOR   Richard Rennert
EXECUTIVE MANAGING EDITOR   Karyn Gullen Browne
COPY CHIEF   Robin James
PICTURE EDITOR   Adrian G. Allen
ART DIRECTOR   Robert Mitchell
MANUFACTURING DIRECTOR   Gerald Levine
PRODUCTION COORDINATOR   Marie Claire Cebrián-Ume

North American Indians of Achievement
SENIOR EDITOR   Marian W. Taylor

Staff for BEN NIGHTHORSE CAMPBELL
ASSISTANT EDITOR   Margaret Dornfeld
EDITORIAL ASSISTANTS   Anne McDonnell, Joy Sanchez
SENIOR DESIGNER   Rae Grant
PICTURE RESEARCHER   Lisa Kirchner
COVER ILLUSTRATOR   Bradford Brown

3   5   7   9   8   6   4   2

Library of Congress Cataloging-in-Publication Data

Henry, Christopher.
Ben Nighthorse Campbell: Cheyenne chief and U.S. senator/Christopher Henry.
    p. cm.—(North American Indians of achievement)
Includes bibliographical references and index.
ISBN 0-7910-2046-0
ISBN 0-7910-2047-9 (pbk.)
1. Campbell, Ben Nighthorse, 1933– . 2.Cheyenne Indians—Biography. 3. Chey-
enne Indians—Kings and rulers. 4. Legislators—United States—Biography. I. Ti-
tle. II. Series.
E99.C53C354 1994   93-27063
973'.04973'0092—dc20   CIP
[B]   AC

CONTENTS

NORTH AMERICAN INDIANS OF ACHIEVEMENT

BLACK HAWK
Sac Rebel

JOSEPH BRANT
Mohawk Chief

BEN NIGHTHORSE CAMPBELL
Cheyenne Chief
and U.S. Senator

COCHISE
Apache Chief

CRAZY HORSE
Sioux War Chief

CHIEF GALL
Sioux War Chief

GERONIMO
Apache Warrior

HIAWATHA
Founder of the
Iroquois Confederacy

CHIEF JOSEPH
Nez Perce Leader

PETER MacDONALD
Former Chairman of
the Navajo Nation

WILMA MANKILLER
Principal Chief of the Cherokees

OSCEOLA
Seminole Rebel

QUANAH PARKER
Comanche Chief

KING PHILIP
Wampanoag Rebel

POCAHONTAS
Powhatan Peacemaker

PONTIAC
Ottawa Rebel

RED CLOUD
Sioux War Chief

WILL ROGERS
Cherokee Entertainer

SITTING BULL
Chief of the Sioux

TECUMSEH
Shawnee Rebel

JIM THORPE
Sac and Fox Athlete

SARAH WINNEMUCCA
Northern Paiute Writer and Diplomat

Other titles in preparation

ON INDIAN LEADERSHIP

by W. David Baird
Howard A. White Professor of History
Pepperdine University

Authoritative utterance is in thy mouth, perception is in thy heart, and thy tongue is the shrine of justice," the ancient Egyptians said of their king. From him, the Egyptians expected authority, discretion, and just behavior. Homer's *Iliad* suggests that the Greeks demanded somewhat different qualities from their leaders: justice and judgment, wisdom and counsel, shrewdness and cunning, valor and action. It is not surprising that different people living at different times should seek different qualities from the individuals they looked to for guidance. By and large, a people's requirements for leadership are determined by two factors: their culture and the unique circumstances of the time and place in which they live.

Before the late 15th century, when non-Indians first journeyed to what is now North America, most Indian tribes were not ruled by a single person. Instead, there were village chiefs, clan headmen, peace chiefs, war chiefs, and a host of other types of leaders, each with his or her own specific duties. These influential people not only decided political matters but also helped shape their tribe's social, cultural, and religious life. Usually, Indian leaders held their positions because they had won the respect of their peers. Indeed, if a leader's followers at any time decided that he or she was out of step with the will of the people, they felt free to look to someone else for advice and direction.

Thus, the greatest achievers in traditional Indian communities were men and women of extraordinary talent. They were not only skilled at navigating the deadly waters of tribal politics and cultural customs but also able to, directly or indirectly, make a positive and significant difference in the daily life of their followers.

From the beginning of their interaction with Native Americans, non-Indians failed to understand these features of Indian leadership. Early European explorers and settlers merely assumed that Indians had the same relationship with their leaders as non-Indians had with their kings and queens. European monarchs generally inherited their positions and ruled large nations however they chose, often with little regard for the desires or needs of their subjects. As a result, the settlers of Jamestown saw Pocahontas as a "princess" and Pilgrims dubbed Wampanoag leader Metacom "King Philip," envisioning them in roles very different from those in which their own people placed them.

As more and more non-Indians flocked to North America, the nature of Indian leadership gradually began to change. Influential Indians no longer had to take on the often considerable burden of pleasing only their own people; they also had to develop a strategy of dealing with the non-Indian newcomers. In a rapidly changing world, new types of Indian role models with new ideas and talents continually emerged. Some were warriors; others were peacemakers. Some held political positions within their tribes; others were writers, artists, religious prophets, or athletes. Although the demands of Indian leadership altered from generation to generation, several factors that determined which Indian people became prominent in the centuries after first contact remained the same.

Certain personal characteristics distinguished these Indians of achievement. They were intelligent, imaginative, practical, daring, shrewd, uncompromising, ruthless, and logical. They were constant in friendships, unrelenting in hatreds, affectionate with their relatives, and respectful to their God or gods. Of course, no single Native American leader embodied all these qualities, nor these qualities only. But it was these characteristics that allowed them to succeed.

The special skills and talents that certain Indians possessed also brought them to positions of importance. The life of Hiawatha, the legendary founder of the powerful Iroquois Confederacy, displays the value that oratorical ability had for many Indians in power.

The biography of Cochise, the 19th-century Apache chief, illustrates that leadership often required keen diplomatic skills not only in transactions among tribespeople but also in hardheaded negotiations with non-Indians. For others, such as Mohawk Joseph Brant and Navajo Peter MacDonald, a non-Indian education proved advantageous in their dealings with other peoples.

Sudden changes in circumstance were another crucial factor in determining who became influential in Indian communities. King Philip in the 1670s and Geronimo in the 1880s both came to power when their people were searching for someone to lead them into battle against white frontiersmen who had forced upon them a long series of indignities. Seeing the rising discontent of Indians of many tribes in the 1810s, Tecumseh and his brother, the Shawnee prophet Tenskwatawa, proclaimed a message of cultural revitalization that appealed to thousands. Other Indian achievers recognized cooperation with non-Indians as the most advantageous path during their lifetime. Sarah Winnemucca in the late 19th century bridged the gap of understanding between her people and their non-Indian neighbors through the publication of her autobiography *Life Among the Piutes*. Olympian Jim Thorpe in the early 20th century championed the assimilationist policies of the U.S. government and, with his own successes, demonstrated the accomplishments Indians could make in the non-Indian world. And Wilma Mankiller, principal chief of the Cherokees, continues to fight successfully for the rights of her people through the courts and through negotiation with federal officials.

Leadership among Native Americans, just as among all other peoples, can be understood only in the context of culture and history. But the centuries that Indians have had to cope with invasions of foreigners in their homelands have brought unique hardships and obstacles to the Native American individuals who most influenced and inspired others. Despite these challenges, there has never been a lack of Indian men and women equal to these tasks. With such strong leaders, it is no wonder that Native Americans remain such a vital part of this nation's cultural landscape.

1

▼▽▼

THE LOST WARRIOR

One summer evening in 1976, Ben Campbell, teacher, craftsman, and deputy sheriff of California's Sacramento County, met with leaders of the Cheyenne nation at a private home in Lame Deer, Montana. Though Lame Deer was—and is—a Native American community, the house where the meeting took place was much like any other American home in 1976. There were no tomahawks, drums, or peace pipes in sight, no tepees nearby, no herds of buffalo on distant hills. The house was equipped with modern appliances and furnished in the style of the times. The people gathered there wore clothing much like that of other Americans and ate food similar to that enjoyed in most American households. Yet these were Cheyenne people, as surely as their grandparents and great-grandparents had been Cheyenne, and on this night their business was to acknowledge that Ben Campbell, too, was a member of the Cheyenne nation.

Though he had spent most of his life far away from Lame Deer and the history and traditions it represented, Campbell was proud of his Cheyenne heritage. Fifty miles to the west of Lame Deer, 100 years earlier, a historic struggle had occurred in which the Cheyennes—Campbell's ancestors among them—had played an important part. At the place now known as the Little Bighorn

Congressman Ben Nighthorse Campbell discusses Indian issues at Fort Lewis College in Durango, Colorado, during Native American Heritage Month, November 1990.

11

Battlefield, a united army of Sioux, Arapaho, and Cheyenne Indians had destroyed General George Armstrong Custer and his entire company of 264 men. The Battle of the Little Bighorn was one of the most devastating defeats the U.S. Army had ever suffered at the hands of an Indian enemy.

For many years, the battle was remembered in books and films as a great American tragedy, with Custer as its hero. The Indians who fought at the Little Bighorn were seen as nameless, faceless obstacles to the truly American cause of westward expansion. The Indians' own losses during the Battle of the Little Bighorn were never

General George Armstrong Custer's Seventh Cavalry clashes with Indian warriors in a pictographic account of the Battle of the Little Bighorn, drawn by a Sioux Indian named Red Horse in 1881. Cheyenne artists produced similar works, usually rendered in paint on canvas or buffalo hide.

considered. In fact, many Indians died in the conflict, itself the product of a long list of irreparable wrongs the United States had committed against the Indians.

Like most other Indian tribes, the Cheyennes had once occupied vast stretches of North American land; like other tribes, they had gradually lost this land as white traders and settlers pushed westward. Despite a series of U.S. government treaties, first promising peaceful relations, then guaranteeing the Indians the right to keep and protect their own lands, settlers continued to spill into Cheyenne territory, spreading disease, disrupting the movement of the buffalo, and generating a chain of violent conflicts. Undaunted by government promises of peace and fair treatment, many settlers abused their right to safe passage to lands farther west, trespassing on Cheyenne hunting grounds and often assaulting those Indians who stood in their way. The Indians retaliated, and as tensions mounted, the U.S. military entered the ring. In 1856, when a series of Cheyenne attacks led to the death of a mail transporter on his way to a U.S. fort, the army responded by arbitrarily killing 10 Cheyennes camped in the surrounding area. In 1857, after further hostilities, a U.S. Army force under Colonel E. V. Sumner attacked a Cheyenne war party on Nebraska's Republican River and killed more than 20 Indians. Finally, in 1864, a force of more than 700 cavalrymen surrounded a Cheyenne encampment at Sand Creek, Colorado, and randomly slaughtered more than 150 men, women, and children. With the Sand Creek massacre, the Cheyenne Indians saw nearly 50 years of U.S. government promises turned to dust. For the Cheyennes, then, the Battle of the Little Bighorn, though certainly a cause for sorrow, was also an act of anger and of protest, and they remembered those who fought it with gravity and respect.

Among the Cheyennes who fought at the Little

Bighorn was an accomplished warrior named Black Horse. Although only 22 years old at the time, he had already become a member of the tribe's most highly revered warrior society, the Dog Soldiers. On the day Custer and his troops met their destiny, Black Horse carried with him a weapon resembling a rough-hewn butcher knife. Its four-inch handle was carved from elk horn, and its blade, which was more than a foot in length, had been fashioned from steel and sharpened on stones. The handle was secured to the blade by an uneven row of nails. It was a primitive weapon, but an effective one, and it served Black Horse well in his struggle against the bluecoats. The young warrior survived the battle, living on to take three wives—a practice not uncommon in Cheyenne culture—to help them raise a family, and to pass his war knife on to other members of the tribe.

Ben Campbell, a mixed-blood Cheyenne, knew from the stories his father had told him that his great-grand-father, a skilled warrior named Black Horse, had helped defeat Custer's men at the Little Bighorn. As he stood among the Cheyenne leaders at Lame Deer, waiting to be accepted into their community, this knowledge—this story that had been passed down three generations, despite the many times his family had confirmed their decision to leave Cheyenne tradition behind—gave him the assurance that he belonged.

The road to Lame Deer had been a long one. Like so many other Native Americans growing up in the 1930s and 1940s, Campbell had drifted through the first few decades of his life bereft of the identity that was his birthright. He had not been raised in an Indian community, but in rural California, where the people came from many backgrounds. Campbell's father, aware that Indian blood was a disadvantage in a prejudiced world, had advised the boy to ignore his Cheyenne heritage, and

Sitting Bull, the head chief of the Teton Sioux from 1867 to 1890, was one of the strongest voices of resistance in the struggle for control of the Great Plains. At the Battle of the Little Bighorn, he led his people to their last victory over the U.S. Army.

although Campbell did not like denying his identity, no one ever encouraged him to do otherwise. In the movies Campbell watched when he was young, Indians were portrayed as cruel, violent, dishonest, cowardly, and primitive. Often they served as comic figures, appearing in absurd costumes and communicating only in grunts or growls. The white men these Indians fought—whether cavalry troops, cowboys, or settlers on wagon trains— seemed brave, clean, honest, intelligent, and God-fearing. Rare was the film in which the "superior" white man did not triumph over the "inferior" Indian. From these images and from those he encountered in schoolbooks, in the games he played with other children, and in everyday conversation, Campbell concluded that it was better not to be an Indian in the white man's world.

Campbell's skin was dark, but because his mother was Portuguese, he could attribute his complexion to his Latin background and "pass" as a non-Indian if he chose to do so. His name gave nothing away. It was not clear how his father had come to be called "Campbell"; Indians who left tribal tradition behind sometimes took the name of an employer or another familiar figure in order to fit in better with white society, and Campbell's relatives may have done the same. In any case, the name's Scottish roots made life convenient for a family of mixed heritage that hoped to be looked on as white. For the most part, then, Ben Campbell was able to go through life like other Americans, keeping his Cheyenne ancestry to himself.

Now, however, having gradually come to know the history and traditions of his people, Campbell wanted more than anything to know in his heart, and for others to know, that he was a Cheyenne. It was a moment he had been working toward for several years, and he recognized its weight.

Campbell knew that the Cheyenne chiefs, in giving him his new identity, would also give him a new name, one that would bind him to the tribe for the rest of his life. Standing before the Cheyenne leaders, he waited for this name. "You will be called Night Horse," they told him. "As your great-grandfather was called." Campbell understood what they were saying. "Black Horse" and "Night Horse" were two English translations of the same Cheyenne name. When written, the name would be spelled as one word: *Nighthorse*.

Ben Nighthorse Campbell, the lost warrior, had become a part of the Cheyenne tribe. He had come home not only to Lame Deer, Montana, where his people lived, but also to his heritage. Later, Cheyenne leaders would present him with an unusual gift, one that they knew he would be proud to claim: a rugged knife with an elkhorn handle, fastened to its steel blade with an irregular row of nails. Campbell would grow quickly in the tribe, and within 10 years he would be called to join the Cheyenne Council of Chiefs. But he would make his mark on the white man's world as well. One day the knife that his great-grandfather had carried into battle at the Little Bighorn would belong to a U.S. senator.

2

AN INDEPENDENT SPIRIT

The life into which Ben Campbell was born on April 13, 1933, in Auburn, California, did not hold much promise for success or happiness. At that time, the nation was still embroiled in the most massive economic depression it had ever witnessed. Throughout the United States, millions of men and women were without a job; many had lost their faith in the country's future. And the Campbell household, it seemed, bore more than its share of the nation's troubles. Ben's parents were so burdened with their own adversities that they had little energy left for their family, and at an early age Ben was forced to abandon the security that most children take for granted.

Ben's father, who was 30 years old when his son was born, was an alcoholic. Albert Campbell was part Cheyenne and probably part Hispanic. Like many Native Americans of his generation, he faced discrimination in school, in work, and in relations with others in his community. Like many others, Albert found in alcohol a brief escape from the pains and pressures of his daily routine. Unfortunately, his efforts to escape ultimately became so frequent and so excessive that they only brought him further hardships, and the turmoil that resulted weighed heavily on his entire family. Unable to

Eighteen-year-old Ben Campbell joined the U.S. Air Force in 1951 and became part of an air police unit in South Korea. He remained in the service until 1953.

19

hold a steady job, at times so drunk he would sleep in the gutter, jailed repeatedly for fighting, stealing, and a myriad of petty offenses, Albert Campbell made day-to-day life difficult for his wife, son, and daughter.

Campbell's drinking problem was so severe that he would sometimes disappear for months at a time, leaving his wife, whose maiden name was Mary Vierra, to fend for herself and the children. Mary, meanwhile, suffered from tuberculosis. The illness would confine her to her

Between the ages of two and four, Ben Campbell often stayed at St. Patrick's Children's Home, pictured here.

bed for long periods, leaving her unable to work or care for her family. Although now treatable with antibiotics, tuberculosis was at that time both widespread and deadly, devastating not only its victims but also their families; it was not uncommon for tubercular parents to have to leave their children for months or years at a time in order to be treated.

As a result of his parents' debilities, Ben and his sister were separated from their mother and father frequently during their early childhood. When he was two years old Ben was sent for the first time to St. Patrick's Children's Home, an institution that cared for orphans and other children who needed extra adult attention. He was able to return home after several weeks, but until he was four years old, each time his parents' troubles increased to a point where they felt they could not cope with a family, he would return to the orphanage for an extended period. His sister, Alberta, who was three years older, also spent time in child-care institutions, sometimes separated from Ben. Left in the hands of strangers, the children felt isolated and unloved, and Ben's experience at St. Patrick's left him with sad and bitter feelings, particularly toward his father. "As an adult, I forgave him for what he did, but I couldn't forget what he did," he later said. "I forgave him because alcoholism is a disease, and he was sick with that disease. But I could never forget what it was like to be placed in that orphanage. It changed my whole life—permanently. Abandonment scars you forever."

Although Ben's father had little formal education and was usually without work, he was neither unintelligent nor unskilled. When he was sober enough to spend time with his son, he would occasionally share with Ben some of the lore of the Cheyenne people. Even though he discouraged the boy from letting others know about his Indian ancestry, he seemed to want his connection with the tribe to be passed on. And Albert taught Ben other things he could never learn in school, such as how to hammer a silver dollar into a piece of Indian jewelry. Ben's father had learned jewelry making from the Navajos, and he would begin by setting a silver dollar on the railroad tracks, which were near the Campbell home, a few minutes before a train was due. Ben and his father would wait patiently until the train had passed, then retrieve the coin, which had been pressed into a large, flat disk—perfect for making a medallion or bracelet.

Unfortunately, these good times were too brief to offset the harm that Albert brought his family through his drinking, unemployment, and prolonged absences. Looking back on his father much later, Ben Campbell would remember him mostly as a source of pain and worry. He recalled, "Sometimes we would have to turn over drunks in Sacramento on skid row to find out which one he was." Perhaps most frightening of all to Ben was the violent energy with which Albert would plow through life when under the influence of alcohol. One of Ben's clearest childhood memories centers on an evening spent with his drunken father in a bar. Albert Campbell got into a fight, and as Ben looked on in horror, his father's opponent stabbed him in the head with an ice pick. To the boy's amazement, Albert, bleeding profusely, with the pick still lodged in his head, "beat the living hell out of the other man" before being taken to a hospital emergency room, where an equally amazed medical staff carefully removed the instrument.

Ben began working at about the age of nine, taking whatever part-time jobs he could get and using the money to help his mother as much as to treat himself. When he was about 13 years old, he started to make friends with a group of Japanese boys that he had met through a job picking fruit. In general, Ben sympathized with other minority-background children, young people whose appearance and family history kept them from being accepted by the larger society. Although physically small and often without much in the way of weight or muscle, the Japanese boys could defend themselves impressively when challenged. Explaining to Ben that they practiced a martial art called judo, they offered to share some of their secrets with him.

Ben found the offer irresistible. What could be more useful for a boy who was alone in the world than to know how to protect himself against those who were bigger and stronger? Campbell threw himself into the project with enthusiasm. His newfound friends would probably have been astonished if they had known how far their limited knowledge of judo would eventually take him; in a few years he would know more about judo than any of them, and a short time after that he would join the ranks of the world's most prominent martial artists.

Ben never particularly cared for classroom studies, but at Auburn's Placer High School he was popular and well respected. His best subjects were art, shop, and physical education, and he played lineman on the school's football team. The students at Placer could be rough and competitive, and Ben's athletic abilities helped him get along. Once, when some older boys started to gang up and intimidate Ben and other students at the school, Ben decided to take the matter into his own hands. He thought it would be better to fight the leader of the gang right at the start—before the group became too tightly organized—than to wait and have to face the whole set of them later. He got the boy to meet him one-on-one, but before either of them could come out ahead a teacher broke up the fight. Ben, however, had achieved his goal; the gang dissolved, and he and his friends had no more trouble. Ben liked to meet his challenges head-on—throughout

his life, his boldness would be one of his greatest strengths.

When he was 17, six months before he was to graduate, Campbell dropped out of high school. Impatient with schoolwork and frustrated with his family, he wanted to head out into the world; he longed for travel, adventure, and good times. And, like thousands of young men before and after him, he found the ideal way of getting to the places he wanted to go: riding the freight trains that barreled across the West. Campbell "rode the rails," slipping onto trains as they waited in stockyards or jumping aboard as they slowed on uphill climbs.

Of course, Campbell had to eat, too. Fortunately, for a strong young man who was willing to accept hard, long hours, physical danger, and low pay, there was plenty of work to be had in the western United States. Campbell took a variety of jobs over the next year, most of them with the timber industry in the Pacific Northwest.

Meanwhile, events in the nation were taking a new turn. The Great Depression had been left behind, World War II had been fought and won, and the United States was enjoying peace and relative prosperity. In June 1950, however, a new crisis emerged: forces from North Korea, now under the protection of the Soviet Union, invaded U.S.-supported South Korea. President Harry Truman demanded immediate action, the draft was reinstated, and U.S. troops were sent overseas.

Early in 1951, just after he turned 18, Ben Campbell enlisted in the U.S. Air Force. For him, as for other men and women with Native American roots, the decision to become a part of the U.S. military had special significance. These volunteers found themselves defending the very government that had gone to war against their ancestors, forcing them to give up their lands and often their way of life. Young recruits such as Campbell had

Campbell relaxes near an aircraft display at a U.S. Air Force base in San Antonio, Texas. Before leaving for Korea, the young airman spent several months on a model-making assignment in the United States.

to search their souls in a special way to come to terms with the relationship. Those Indians who chose to serve often did so with courage and distinction, however, some of them bringing unusual skills to the armed services.

During World War II, Navajo recruits played a crucial role in the operations of the U.S. Navy. Familiar with the language of their parents and grandparents, these men were able to relay radio communications between ships in a "code" that was entirely unknown to the Japanese counterintelligence specialists. When the Navajos began to communicate in their own language, the Japanese analysts were stymied—no code-breaking chart could help them.

When Campbell entered the air force, it was his skill as a craftsman that the military first put to work. After basic training, he began an assignment as a model maker, remaining in the United States for his first few months of service. The air force used small-scale models as engineering mock-ups for the early stages of aircraft construction; larger models were introduced to artificial wind tunnels for aerodynamic testing, and others were created for display. Campbell's technical skill suited him well for the careful work of model construction, but recruits were still needed abroad, and eventually he was transferred to an air police unit and shipped to Korea.

The Korean War took a harsh toll on the U.S. armed services. Of the nearly 6 million men and women who served there, more than 54,000 died and more than 100,000 were wounded. Like all war, the Korean War had a devastating emotional impact on those who witnessed its violence. Campbell was never assigned to combat, but 40 years after he left Korea he vividly remembered the horrors he had seen there: "I saw legless children in blood-soaked rags, pulling themselves along the roads with their arms, using their hands to claw themselves forward a few feet at a time past the bombed-out buildings that were once homes and factories. If there was one thing I learned in Korea, it's what wars do to kids."

The air force gave Campbell the opportunity to explore more of the United States as well as Asia. Over the course of his military career, he was stationed at various times in Panama City, Florida; Amarillo, Texas; and Las Vegas, Nevada. Honorably discharged in 1953, he was immediately offered a job as a patrolman in the Las Vegas Police Department. Campbell was tempted by the offer; a police force job would mean a solid career with good pay and room to advance. But all that considered, there were other things that Campbell wanted more. He turned down the offer and headed home to California.

3

▽▽▽

A MASTER OF THE ART

Throughout Campbell's early life, he dreamed of mastering the art of judo. After his boyhood friends had shown him what they could do with their small battery of self-defense moves, he knew there was a new world he wanted to explore.

The first Asian martial art to become popular in the United States, judo was derived from a more violent form of unarmed combat called jujitsu, which was practiced in Japan from the 12th century onward. One of the fundamental principles of both judo and jujitsu is that a person who is smaller or weaker than an attacker can nevertheless win in a conflict by taking advantage of the opponent's own size, strength, and momentum.

This defensive tactic is by no means unique to the martial arts of Asia. In the 19th century, Native Americans used it successfully against U.S. troops: Indian bands would sometimes draw a large army into an area where its very size and strength would reduce its mobility and effectiveness. Although the heavy artillery and the store of munitions that accompanied white armies could be devastating in extended combat, they served no purpose when the troops were taken by surprise; they merely

Ben Campbell flips an opponent at a 1961 college judo match.

29

prevented the soldiers' quick escape. Indian war bands also knew how to gain an advantage over their more powerful enemies by appearing weaker—or stronger— than they really were. Such tactics, like those of judo, relied more heavily on reasoning and rapid planning than on physical strength.

Campbell first learned judo for practical reasons. He lived in a troubled, often hostile world, and he could see that judo was an effective and efficient form of self-defense. But he soon decided that the martial art also had a strong mental—even philosophical—dimension. As he saw it, judo students developed not only their muscles but also their powers of concentration; they adopted an attitude of respect toward themselves and toward their opponents. Devoted practitioners—people who made judo the focus of their lives—often found that the principles they learned from it could be applied to all of their activities and decisions. Perhaps the discipline judo required and the philosophical guidance it offered were just the stabilizing influences that the restless Campbell needed.

While Campbell was in the air force he had earned a General Equivalency Diploma, which made him an official high school graduate. After returning to California in 1953 he worked as a field hand for about a year. Harvesting and loading fruits and vegetables was hot, dirty, and tiring. Most of Campbell's coworkers were members of minority groups, people whose poor education prevented them from being hired elsewhere. Wages were low, and farm workers—at that time without a union to protect them—were forced to accept whatever conditions their employers offered them.

Campbell nevertheless managed to save enough money to move on, and in 1954 he entered San Jose City College. "I wanted to go to San Jose State, but that wasn't possible," Campbell later recalled. "Because I hadn't earned a regular high school diploma, the folks at San Jose State wanted to see something in the way of good grades before they would consider admitting me." He proved himself in two semesters and transferred in 1955 to San Jose State University, where, two years earlier, the first national judo championships had been held. Campbell made sure that judo would be a central part of his course of study.

Although government education aid was available to Korean War veterans, Campbell's study grant did not go very far, and unlike younger classmates, who could turn to their parents for help, he had to support himself. To do that, he learned to drive an 18-wheeler and worked his way through four years of college. Like other truck drivers, Campbell joined the Teamsters union, an alliance that was rapidly becoming one of the most powerful labor organizations in the nation. Though a number of Teamsters officials would later be convicted of racketeering and other crimes, most members of the union in Campbell's time were ordinary men trying to keep food on their families' tables, and Campbell appreciated their solidarity.

At San Jose State, Campbell joined the judo team, and under fifth-degree black belt coach Yosh Uchida, he made fast progress. In 1957, the team won the California State championship, and in the same competition Campbell was awarded with an individual crown. Later Campbell, as cocaptain, led the team to victory in the Novice and Senior Black Belt divisions of the Amateur Athletic Union Pacific Championships. Campbell was the Pacific AAU heavyweight champion that year, and he placed second in the Castle Air Force Base Invitational Tournament, one of the largest judo tournaments in the nation. By the time he graduated, he ranked as a third-degree black belt.

Juggling a schedule that included a full-time job,

full-time studies, and the rigorous physical regimen that went with his devotion to judo, Campbell completed a bachelor's degree in physical education and fine arts in 1957. After graduation he began a master's program at San Jose State; more interested in his judo career than in his studies, however, he left the program during his second year. Throughout his university career, Campbell's preoccupation with judo had remained unshaken; his athletic perseverance, as it turned out, was soon to be rewarded.

Seven years after his discharge from the U.S. Air Force, Campbell, his aims redefined, returned to Asia. Most of the people with whom he had served were happy to leave Korea, return to the United States, and leave their Asian experience behind them for good. But Campbell had his ambition to attend to. In 1960 he settled in Tokyo, Japan, the country where judo originated, and began attending Meiji University as a postgraduate research student. Campbell's real aim, of course, was to further develop his skills in the art of judo; in Japan, where the martial art was as commonplace as basketball was in the United States, he knew he could really grow.

Campbell lived in Japan for the next four years, training five hours a day, six days a week. Over the course of his stay he broke his nose nine times and knocked out two teeth. From time to time he traveled to the United States and other parts of the world to participate in judo competitions. He supported himself during these years in a number of ways: teaching English, playing bit parts in French and German films, and even teaching judo to Japanese students. Campbell discovered he was a good teacher; not only was he proficient in his subject but he seemed to have a natural talent for passing his knowledge on to others, despite the English-Japanese language barrier.

Campbell sits for an interview after winning the gold medal at the Pan-American Games.

Between training and work, Campbell had little time for other interests, but he nevertheless began to pursue a side activity during his stay in Tokyo. Not far from his apartment lived a samurai-sword craftsman whom he liked to visit. Campbell noticed similarities between the artistic skills required to make a samurai sword and those he had used as a boy when making Indian jewelry. The sword maker also taught him a special Japanese metalworking technique. The ancient process involved inlaying various colored metals—such as copper or brass—and could be used to create designs of great strength, beauty, and durability. Campbell would eventually introduce to the United States a variation on traditional Indian jewelry—one that incorporated the lamination technique he learned from his Japanese friend.

As he polished his skills, Campbell began to establish himself in the world of martial arts. Having struggled forward inch by inch, he was finally reaping the rewards. Campbell became a heavyweight champion in the U.S. Open judo competition in 1961, then repeated his performance in 1962 and 1963. He won a gold medal at the 1963 Pan-American Games in São Paulo, Brazil. Though he claimed Japan as his place of residence, at international events he always represented the United States, and in 1964 he was named an All-American at the U.S. Open and captain of the U.S. Olympic team for the games to be held in Tokyo that year. The site had been chosen years earlier, and Campbell had probably hoped when he moved to Tokyo in 1960 that he would compete there in the 1964 Olympics. Though the team came away from the games without a medal—Campbell was injured in the second round—its captain knew he had come far, and he lost none of his enthusiasm for the discipline.

After coaching the U.S. International Judo Team for a season, Campbell moved back to the United States and resettled in the Sacramento Valley. He found a job teaching junior high school in the San Juan school district and while there set up a course for physical education teachers on how to teach judo to their students. Linda

Campbell takes a walk with his father, Albert Campbell, and the family dog in 1964.

Price, a rancher's daughter from Montrose, Colorado, enrolled in the course, and she and Campbell soon became friends. "We were both sports nuts," he recalled. "She had been very active on her college ski team. We had a lot in common." Campbell had tried his hand at marriage twice before, once in 1957, when he finished college, and again while he was training for the Olympics in Japan; neither of these relationships had lasted for more than a few months. With Linda, however, Campbell had a feeling he had found the right companion, and in 1966 they married. Unlike his previous marriages, this one seemed made to last, and within a few years Ben and Linda Campbell would have a daughter, Shanan, and a son, Colin.

Ben Campbell and Linda Price pause for a snapshot next to Campbell's new Jaguar in 1964. Campbell met his wife, a fellow sports enthusiast, at the junior high school where he was working at the time.

Meanwhile, Campbell was expanding his career as a judo instructor. To supplement his regular teaching job, he became the host of a public television program on women's self-defense, a show that remained on the air until 1966. Campbell also opened a small private school where he taught judo to children.

Two of Campbell's students at the judo school were the sons of Duane Lowe, then a candidate for sheriff of Sacramento County. Lowe won the election and was sworn into office early in 1971. The sheriff would take his sons to judo class two or three times a week, and he and Campbell gradually came to be friends. The two men came from similar backgrounds: Lowe had grown up dirt-poor on an Oklahoma farm, quit school when he was

16, and headed off on his own to Montana, where he harvested wheat before joining the navy.

Lowe was always impressed by the way Campbell handled his students. "Ben Campbell was a perfect role model for young men," he later remembered. "He had impeccable character, tremendous physical prowess and stature, and expert skills in hand-to-hand combat." Suspecting that he had found a natural leader, Lowe soon offered Campbell a job as a deputy sheriff with the county; he knew his friend was an excellent horseman, and he hoped to place him at the head of a mounted police unit.

Accepting the offer, Campbell became a Sacramento County deputy sheriff in 1972. Shortly afterward he and Lowe traveled to New York City, where the mounted unit of the New York Police Department taught them the basics of horseback law enforcement. The New York police had come to consider horses indispensable: at public events mounted police were in a better position to control crowds, and they could move quickly into terrain where cars were impractical. Though Lowe's territory was less urban, his officers had many of the same needs as the New York force; in the parks of Sacramento County, drug dealing and other crimes were on the rise.

On their return, Lowe and Campbell set up Sacramento County's first mounted police unit. Lowe's budget for the venture was small, so Campbell and the other officers provided their own horses. The sheriff was well satisfied with the result. Along with its advantages as a law-enforcement tool, the unit made the Sacramento County force more visible, and with Campbell at its head Lowe felt it created an image of integrity and competence. "Ben Campbell was an excellent peace officer, a truly humane law-enforcement professional," he recalled later. "In his bearing, he was the epitome of a military officer. Back

Campbell takes care of paperwork at the Sacramento County sheriff's office, where he served as deputy sheriff from 1972 to 1977.

then he had close-cropped hair, like a marine's, and looked you right in the eye when he addressed you. He was unpretentious, but outstanding."

Campbell found police work challenging, both physically and emotionally. Although he enjoyed his public role and the companionship of his fellow officers, his tasks, like those of any police officer, sometimes felt like a burden. On one occasion, Campbell was called on to help break up a fight that had broken out in a neighborhood bar. The job meant arresting the son of an Indian friend of his, and the young man refused to go peacefully—it took eight officers to bring him in. Some time after the incident, the man he arrested—who was involved in drugs—committed suicide.

Campbell's training in the martial arts had taught him to treat his opponents with respect, and he tried to apply the same philosophy in his job as deputy sheriff. With this in mind, in addition to his duties as a mounted officer, he taught judo at the county's police academy. He hoped the lessons would help other officers deal with violent situations defensively, using a minimum of force. Meanwhile, throughout his career in law enforcement Campbell was reminded repeatedly of the disadvantages faced by people of Native American descent—of the obstacles they had to surmount in order to live productive, peaceful lives. In his free hours, he sometimes offered counseling to the Indian inmates of Sacramento County's Folsom prison.

While he was acting as deputy sheriff, Campbell became more interested in working with his hands, and once again he took up his boyhood hobby of making jewelry. Before long he was pursuing this side interest with almost as much zeal as he had shown when learning judo, and he began entering Indian jewelry shows and competitions. Campbell's lapidary work—which followed a long tradition of inlaying semiprecious stones in gold or silver—was generally well received. When he started using the lamination techniques he had learned in Japan, however, the Indian art establishment at first resisted, arguing that his pieces were inauthentic. Campbell had a different attitude. After all, it was from the Spanish that the Navajos had first learned to make silver jewelry; it seemed to Campbell that incorporating other "outside" influences was just a way of allowing the tradition to evolve. Eventually the art community came around. In the early 1970s, Campbell won one of his first jewelry awards for a bracelet and necklace he made from silver and abalone shell. When he entered his works at the California State Fair, he won the top prize over thousands of other artists, becoming the first jeweler of Indian ancestry to do so. Once again, Campbell had found a new calling, and one that would ultimately strengthen his identity as a member of the Cheyenne tribe.

4

CLOSER TO LAME DEER

The adversities that Ben Campbell had faced early in life and the challenges he met as he matured had made him tough and self-reliant. His sister, Alberta, was not so strong; in 1974 she died from a combined overdose of drugs and alcohol. Like her father—for whom she was named—she remained unable to hold down a steady job or keep a marriage together. Campbell himself could probably not have explained why his own life had taken such a different course.

At the time of his sister's death, Campbell was deeply involved in his new vocation and beginning to make his mark as a designer of Indian jewelry. As Campbell's craftsmanship evolved, he gradually acquired a standing in the Native American art world that rivaled his position in the martial arts. During the 1970s, he won award after award for the sleek, simple, and beautiful designs he made from the metals (both silver and gold) and stones (usually turquoise) that were native to the American West. Campbell's jewelry was unconventional, but always connected to tradition; he drew inspiration from Navajo and

Throughout the 1970s, Campbell's career as a jewelry designer continued to evolve. These works— a pair of bracelets and a belt buckle—exhibit both the lamination technique he learned in Japan and traditional Indian motifs.

other Indian motifs. Some of his pieces incorporated images from petroglyphs—ancient animal designs carved in rock in many parts of the American Southwest. In the course of his artistic career Campbell would win more than 200 prizes; from the critics of his craft he would earn acclaim as one of the country's outstanding Native American artists.

Campbell's career as a designer and craftsman—which brought him into regular contact with other men and women of Native American descent and encouraged him to examine the traditions they shared—went hand-in-hand with a shift in his feelings toward his own Cheyenne heritage. In the early 1970s he began making yearly trips to the Northern Cheyenne reservation in Lame Deer, Montana, and as he visited with leaders there his identification with the tribe increased.

As a Cheyenne, Campbell knew that he was part of a people with a long and troubled history. Although the leaders at Lame Deer had always called Montana home, the Cheyenne tribe had once lived in another part of the

Campbell, by his early forties a prize-winning maker of Indian jewelry, inspects a bracelet in his workshop.

country; it was only over the course of many years of complex, often hostile relations with the U.S. government and its white citizens that the tribe had formed its small community on the broad Montana prairie.

Campbell knew that when the Cheyennes first encountered white people, around 1700, they were living in the region now known as Minnesota. At that time, a number of tribes in the area entered trade agreements with the whites, supplying furs in exchange for metal tools and other manufactured goods. Though peaceful in themselves, these agreements eventually disrupted relations between the tribes who took part in them. In time the competition led to bloodshed, and in order to escape the violence many tribes decided to leave their lands and seek peace farther west. The Cheyennes became a part of this migration in the middle of the 18th century.

The move from Minnesota changed Cheyenne life forever. In their new, less fertile surroundings the Indians could no longer support themselves by farming, and they came to depend on the buffalo for survival. Instead of setting up a permanent home in the West, the tribe broke up into smaller bands and led a nomadic life, following the buffalo herds across the plains. Some bands followed the buffalo southwest into present-day Colorado and Kansas; others continued to hunt in the Dakotas. Eventually, these two groups became known as the Southern and the Northern Cheyennes.

It was during this phase of their history that the Cheyennes and the whites went to war. Throughout the Cheyennes' migrations, which lasted well into the 1800s, white traders were also, little by little, making their way across the Mississippi and onto the Great Plains. In 1825 Cheyenne leaders signed their first treaty with the United States, each side pledging peace and friendship. The agreement held for a while, but toward the middle of the

A 19th-century engraving shows Indians attacking a herd of buffalo. Once the Cheyennes had left their original home in Minnesota, they began to depend on the buffalo for food, and they would follow the herds as they drifted from place to place across the western prairies.

19th century, as settlers and gold miners began traveling across Cheyenne territory, relations between whites and Indians became more hostile. In 1851 the U.S. government drew up a treaty establishing the borders of Cheyenne-Arapaho territory; U.S. leaders hoped to maintain peace by keeping whites and Indians separate. But the government had little control over its citizens in the West. Many whites disregarded the Indians' rights, and a series of violent conflicts followed. Plagued by land-hungry settlers, the U.S. Army, and unfamiliar diseases—another affliction that came with the white invasion—the Northern Cheyennes finally sold the United States a large portion of their land in exchange for a reservation along the Laramie River in southeastern Wyoming. In 1860, the following year, the Southern Cheyennes followed suit, accepting a reservation just north of the Arkansas River in Kansas and Oklahoma. The land the Indians were given was too arid to support them, however, and the fighting did not end.

After the Sand Creek massacre, in 1864, no treaty could persuade the Cheyenne warriors to lay down their arms. Across the western prairies, the Indians continued to raid white settlements, and U.S. military forces retaliated. In 1868 an army regiment laid waste to an encampment of Cheyennes at Oklahoma's Washita River; the following year U.S. troops stormed a Southern Cheyenne village in Nebraska, killing 52 Indians. Meanwhile, the Cheyennes' lands were still slipping out from under them. In the 1870s, when a railroad company sent surveyors out to Southern Cheyenne country, the Indians renewed their attacks, but before long U.S. forces had harassed them into submission.

It was the Northern Cheyennes who were still holding onto their freedom when the young Civil War veteran George Armstrong Custer and his Seventh Cavalry moved in for their attack at the Little Bighorn River. The government had tried to get the Northern Cheyennes to give up the lands they had been granted and move to Oklahoma, but they had refused. When gold was discovered in the Black Hills, a part of Cheyenne territory, and the Indians still would not sell their lands, U.S. officials sent in troops to force them out. Custer, fighting under General Alfred Terry, was a part of this effort.

In June 1876 Terry ordered Custer and his men to follow the Rosebud Creek westward toward the Little Bighorn River Valley, where the Cheyennes and their Sioux and Arapaho allies had their camps. Custer had orders to wait for Terry before taking action, but when the young general caught sight of the smoke rising from the Indians' camp he recklessly forged ahead. Dividing his men into three units, he ordered one group to stay behind and scout the area, another to attack the camp from the southern side, and the third to follow his lead, assaulting the camp from the north. Custer gravely underestimated the size of the Indian encampment. The second unit attacked and was quickly forced to retreat; Custer and his men rode into the camp and faced the Indians alone. The Battle of the Little Bighorn, in which more than 250 U.S. soldiers lost their lives, lasted less than an hour.

It was to be the Cheyennes' final victory. Shamed and infuriated by Custer's defeat, the U.S. Army pursued them into the hills, where they suffered a bitter winter. By 1877 most of the tribe had surrendered, and that summer the government forced about 1,000 Northern Cheyennes to walk across the sun-baked plains to Oklahoma. Two-thirds of the Indians died along the way; the rest joined the Southern Cheyennes and struggled to make a life for themselves on the humid flatlands of their reservation.

In 1878 a group of more than 300 Northern Cheyennes,

unable to adapt to life in Oklahoma, escaped to the north. U.S. troops soon set out after them, and when they reached Nebraska, some members of the group were ready to surrender. At Fort Robinson, where they turned themselves in, they were kept in an unheated prison without food or water for seven days, and many of them died of exposure. Those who continued north finally gave up their weapons to U.S. posts in Wyoming and Montana. In 1884, these Indians were given a small reservation along the Tongue River—close to the area where the Northern Cheyennes were living when Campbell came to know them.

Meanwhile, the Cheyennes who remained in Oklahoma had to leave their old way of life, based on the buffalo hunt, and learn to farm and raise cattle. When their crops failed, they lived on government handouts. In 1887 the U.S. government's allotment policy, which required Indian reservations to be divided into small, one-family tracts, robbed the Southern Cheyennes of still more of their lands. After each family had received its allotment, a large area of the Cheyenne reservation remained; the government pressured the Indians into selling this land so that white farmers could settle it.

Government officials not only obliged the Cheyennes to farm the way white people did, they also tried to make them think and act like whites. In the 1890s a Cheyenne agent outlawed the Sun Dance, one of the tribe's most important sacred ceremonies. By the beginning of the 20th century, many Cheyennes wore white-style clothing, lived in white-style homes, and had given up most of their old traditions.

The Northern Cheyennes, who survived on game and wild fruits for several years, also gradually took up farming. They found they could get by on their own crops, but they fared even better when they began to

U.S. troops travel to the Black Hills on an 1874 exploratory expedition.

breed livestock—first horses, then cattle as well. In 1919, to the Indians' dismay, U.S. officials—who had at first encouraged their ranching venture—decided that the Cheyennes' horses were grazing in areas that should have been reserved for cattle. Government agents came to the reservation and sold or shot most of the horses; in a few years the number of horses owned by the Cheyennes was reduced from 15,000 to 3,000. In the 1920s the Northern Cheyenne reservation, like the land of the Cheyennes to the south, was divided into allotments, and the Indians once again lost more of their property.

From the early 20th century on, many Cheyennes chose to leave reservation life and make their way in the world of the whites. Some worked for white farmers; others sought employment in cities. The lives of these Indians sometimes took them far away from the fields of Oklahoma and Montana. Many of them married outside the tribe and raised children outside the Cheyenne tradition. Campbell's father came from a family that had drifted away from traditional life; there were many others like him.

The Southern Cheyennes who stayed on their reservation continued to live in relative poverty even during Campbell's time, but the Northern Cheyennes had found a way to improve their lives. In the 1960s they had learned that their land contained coal deposits, and they were able to add to their income by doing business with mining companies. They still faced problems; those who ran the mining companies knew the Cheyennes had little business experience, and some of them dealt with them dishonestly. The Indians also had to fight to prevent the companies from strip-mining their lands. Fortunately, by this time the Cheyennes had gained some allies.

Campbell's reintroduction to the Cheyenne world coincided with the emergence in the United States of a

Tombstones commemorate fallen U.S. soldiers at the site of the Battle of the Little Bighorn. In 1976, when Campbell and other Native Americans came to this spot to observe the battle's hundred-year anniversary, the U.S. Park Service refused to let them enter the park without a police escort.

reevaluation of the Native American experience. During the 1960s, the American counterculture had begun to take an interest in Indian traditions, and a political movement supporting Indian rights had started to take shape. In 1968, two important groups, the American Indian Movement and the United Native Americans, were founded. These organizations, endorsed by student and other minority groups, led public demonstrations on issues ranging from land disputes to discrimination in employment. But as late as the mid-1970s, Native Americans had still not achieved any real influence in American politics, and in the rural United States, where many Indians lived and worked, many of the old stereotypes—of laziness, dishonesty, and hopeless alcoholism—persisted. Campbell became part of a widespread effort to reclaim for the Cheyenne and other tribes the respect he felt they deserved.

In the summer of 1976, the year he became a member of the Cheyenne tribe, Campbell traveled to a meeting place near the site of the Battle of the Little Bighorn, where several hundred Native Americans were preparing a memorial service to mark the centennial of the Indian victory over Custer. Campbell and the others had not come to gloat over their ancestors' conquests but to pray and remember those Indian warriors who had died on the battlefield. When they neared the grounds of the Custer Battlefield, as it was then called, they soon found themselves surrounded by U.S. Park Service police. Only in the company of these men—under armed guard, in other words—were they allowed onto the grounds that had once been theirs and were still sacred to them. Meanwhile, all of the other people visiting the battlefield that day—mainly white tourists—were allowed to view the grounds without supervision. One hundred years after the last great Indian victory over the United States government, the U.S. Park Service was still treating Native Americans—including Ben Campbell, a Korean War veteran and a law enforcement officer—like second-class citizens. Campbell, enraged, swore an oath that day: "By God, if I ever can, I will change this!"

5

THE MAVERICK POLITICIAN

In the mid-1970s, Ben and Linda Campbell began to think about moving away from the Sacramento Valley. Both Campbell and his son, Colin, suffered from asthma, and the region—with its heat and smog and especially the smoke that came from the burning of rice stubble (what remains of rice plants after a harvest)—was making life increasingly unpleasant for them. Campbell and his wife were also concerned about raising their children in an area where violent crime and drug use were becoming more common. The Campbells had been doing well financially for the past several years. Linda had continued to work as a teacher, and Ben, between his judo school and his jewelry sales (some of his pieces sold for thousands of dollars), was bringing in a healthy income. In 1977 they decided to pull up roots and move to Colorado, Linda's home state, where they bought a ranch in Ignacio, a small town near the New Mexico border and the Southern Ute Indian reservation.

In his new surroundings, Campbell developed a more relaxed personal style. Exchanging the close-cropped

Ben and Linda Campbell relax with their children, Shanan and Colin, on the porch of their Ignacio, Colorado, ranch house.

55

haircut for a ponytail, he immersed himself in a wide variety of activities, some professional, others for recreation. He continued to teach judo, and in time he came to own a chain of five summer judo camps for children. He made jewelry, as before, finding new inspiration in the landscape around his home. Concentrating with renewed energy on the lamination methods he had been working on over the years, he developed a style he called Painted Mesa, after the many-colored sands of the American Southwest. In 1983 he entered a concha belt executed in this style in the prestigious Gallup Intertribal Ceremonial art show. The belt won first place, best of division, and the Most Creative Metalsmith award, estab-

In 1977, the Campbells moved to Colorado, the state that Linda Campbell's ancestors had settled 100 years earlier. Eventually the couple embellished the driveway to their home with this 16-foot-high gate, built by a friend of Ben Campbell's in exchange for some custom-made jewelry.

lishing the Painted Mesa style as a major contribution to the history of Native American art. Meanwhile, with the many acres of open space now at his disposal, Campbell started breeding quarter horses. Another hobby, motorcycling, was an activity he had enjoyed since the age of 18; in Colorado, he allowed it to expand, taking his Harley-Davidson—his favorite make—to rallies whenever he could fit them into his schedule. Campbell compared the biking world to the culture of Native Americans. He told an interviewer, "[Bikers] love freedom, are clannish in their associations, and enjoy the nomadic lifestyle. Bikers used to be gang guys, but now they're mainly good guys, and highly successful people, most of them." Campbell

The eagle, an important symbol in both European and Indian cultures, figures prominently in a silver belt buckle Campbell made for Colorado senator Gary Hart in 1984, when Hart was running for president. Campbell sold 50 copies of the buckle to help raise money for Hart's campaign.

also enjoyed flying, a skill he had learned in 1976, at the age of 43; in Colorado he had his own plane.

In a way, it was through his interest in flying that Campbell first became involved in politics. Late on a cloudy afternoon in the winter of 1982, he decided to take a trip in his plane—one that would keep him busy for the rest of the evening—and he headed for the small airport where the plane was garaged. On his way he noticed that the weather was not in his favor and looked like it might get worse. By the time he had reached the airport, warmed up the plane's engine, and taxied out to the runway, he realized that he had picked the wrong day. Flying was too risky; he parked his plane and headed home. Looking for another enjoyable way to spend the

A 1982 photograph shows Ben and Linda Campbell enjoying the open spaces of their Colorado property. The 120-acre ranch gave the couple room to breed cattle and quarter horses.

evening, he remembered a story in the local newspaper concerning a meeting that was to be held that night in Durango, a nearby town. The main purpose of the meeting was to select the Democratic party's candidate for the local seat in the Colorado House of Representatives. Campbell knew that a friend of his, Al Brown, was running for sheriff, so he decided to attend the meeting and lend Brown whatever support he could.

It became evident to Campbell soon after he arrived at the meeting that none of the Democrats there thought they had a chance of winning the election. The Republican candidate, a local college administrator named Don Whalen, had outstanding credentials, and they considered him unbeatable. For the sake of appearance, if nothing else, the Democrats had to put forth a candidate, but no one was showing much enthusiasm. Those assembled at the meeting had an unusual job; rather than having to choose between a number of eager candidates, they had to persuade someone—anyone—to run.

That night the candidacy was offered to, and refused by, three local Democrats. The people at the meeting were getting desperate; perhaps the Democratic party would not mount a campaign after all. Some people privately thought they would be better off without a candidate, as there was no chance of winning anyway.

Then someone suggested Ben Campbell. Tall, good-looking, smart, and likable, he would, the assembled Democrats agreed, make as plausible a candidate as anyone. What was more, Campbell, who was new to politics, might not realize that he had no chance of winning the election, and he might actually be persuaded to accept the nomination. If that happened the meeting would be over, and they could all go home. On election day the egg would be on Ben Campbell's face—not theirs.

The plan worked. Flattered by their confidence in him,

Ben Campbell accepted the Democratic nomination for the local seat in the Colorado House of Representatives. His friend Sam Maynes, a local attorney who was also present at the gathering, approached him as the meeting ended. Campbell would remember their conversation for a long time.

"Do you think you can win, Ben?" Maynes asked.

"I don't know," Campbell replied. "What kind of chances do you think I have?"

"You've got two chances, Ben," Maynes replied dryly. "Slim and none."

That night changed Campbell's life forever. Looking back on it later, he reflected:

> Aerodynamic engineers say that it's impossible for bumblebees to fly, but they do fly. Maybe that's because the bumblebees don't know that they can't fly. Well, I didn't know that I couldn't win that election, and I certainly wouldn't have accepted the nomination if I really felt that I couldn't win. I thought I could win it—that's why I ran.

On election day in November 1982, Campbell proved all of the "experts" wrong, defeating Don Whalen by a small but decisive margin. Whalen, the former dean of education at Fort Lewis College in Durango, thought highly of Campbell, who, he said, was "fiscally conservative, and a centrist." Campbell's opponent attributed the upset victory to an exceptionally well-organized campaign, to Campbell's personal popularity in the region, and to his natural abilities as a coalition builder.

At the age of 49, then, Ben Campbell—field hand, truck driver, mounted policeman, craftsman, and motorcycle enthusiast—took up yet another calling—that of an elected official. Blunt and opinionated, he was completely different from most other politicians, many of whom would say or do anything to win an election. Many of Campbell's opponents, and some of his friends, thought his career in politics would be limited to one term, maybe two, in the Colorado House of Representatives. But Campbell's political life, they would discover, had just begun.

From the day he was sworn into office, Campbell wanted to let the voters know that he was his own man—not some puppet of the Democratic party leadership. He had one concern, he said: to represent the people of his district to the best of his abilities. Although a lifelong Democrat, Campbell had never taken voting instructions from anyone. Many people believed that such independence could be fatal to a newly elected politician, but in Campbell's case, it would prove his greatest strength.

In Denver, Campbell seemed to vote with the Republicans as often as he did with the Democrats. As it turned out, this practice made him no less popular with the people in his electoral district; their concerns had little to do with party affiliation. Campbell's home district was rural, in a state that was slowly becoming more urban and industrialized. It was on environmental issues that Campbell most often took the Republicans' side, and his constituents approved.

Campbell loved the land; he had always lived close to it, and he considered it an indispensable part of his life. But he had different views about environmentalists. Defending the interests of those whose jobs depended on land access, he objected to proposals that would limit the use of federal lands by private individuals and organizations. As he once explained, "People in the East and in California think of the National Parks as a place to hike and camp, but that's only a small part of what the acreage in the National Parks has been used for. For many westerners, the National Parks are a place to earn a living."

Campbell's views on the environment may not fit a certain popular image of the Native American—the

image of the gentle lover of nature; Campbell himself believed that many Indians had, in fact, suffered at the hands of "radical environmentalists." For some time the "politics of water" had created a number of bitter conflicts, with those who wished to preserve the landscape on one side of the battle, and those who desperately needed water—water that, it was said, could only be provided by building dams and flooding large areas—on the other. Since Indians were among those who were meant to be served by such water projects, Campbell saw the environmentalists' campaign against the projects as a threat to the Indians' well-being. The environmentalists, Campbell said, seemed willing to break treaties the government had made with Indian tribes if they perceived a risk to the environment. "Of course Indians care about preserving the environment," he once told an interviewer. "We were doing this for hundreds of years before the white man ever set foot in North America. But we also care about jobs, about providing for our families. We can't do that if we can't use our own lands as we see fit."

Consumer issues also became an important part of Campbell's work in the Colorado House. The 1980s, a decade of rapid economic growth in most parts of the United States, saw the proliferation of a large variety of new businesses in the state of Colorado. Of particular concern to Campbell was the widespread emergence of health clubs and spas whose customers were required to pay in advance for as much as a year of service. These fledgling operations were often unstable, and when they failed, their customers—in principle entitled to long-term use of the club—usually lost out. Campbell, who had run into problems with his own club, was determined to see to it that he and other consumers got what they had paid for, and he created a measure requiring health club

State representative Ben Campbell, a man whose political boldness quickly impressed voters across the state, presents his views during a session of the Colorado legislature.

owners who were closing their business either to return their customers' money or have another club take over the contracts that had not yet expired.

Between his legislative duties and his many other activities, Campbell sometimes found it hard to fit everything he wanted to accomplish into his cramped schedule, and on one occasion his conflicting interests got him into trouble. Campbell was thinking about buying a plane he had heard about in Craig, a small community in northwest Colorado. Unfortunately, the time he picked to test-fly the plane was the day the Colorado House was scheduled to vote on a proposed increase in the state's gasoline tax. When speaker of the house Carl Bledsoe discovered that Campbell was absent, he suspended the vote and had Campbell tracked down and instructed to return immediately. Campbell hurried back to Denver, voted against the tax, and accepted with grace the $20 penalty that Bledsoe charge him for his absence.

Generally, Campbell received good ratings during his tenure in the Colorado House of Representatives, both from his constituents, who reelected him in 1984, and from the people of Colorado as a whole. A man who stated his mind and accepted the consequences, Ben Nighthorse Campbell, with his ponytail, western boots, cowboy hat, and bolo ties, was often compared to the popular American humorist and entertainer Will Rogers. Campbell's natural warmth and friendly disposition made him the sort of man who could tell another person that he or she was entirely wrong about an issue without causing any personal offense. Campbell certainly had some detractors, but during his four years in the Colorado House he was also named Outstanding Legislator by the Colorado Bankers' Association and 1984 Man of the Year by the La Plata Farm Bureau. In 1986, the *Denver Post* and a local television station both chose him as one of the 10

A photograph from the Durango Herald *captures Campbell in the throes of his 1986 congressional campaign.*

best legislators in the state. Clearly, Ben Campbell was doing something right in Colorado.

Meanwhile, in 1985, nine years after pronouncing him a member of the Northern Cheyenne tribe, the Council of Chiefs at Lame Deer asked Campbell if he would join their inner circle. Campbell did not accept their invitation without careful thought. He was being asked to make a lifetime commitment. Although the Northern Cheyenne Council of Chiefs had no legal power over the tribe's members, they exercised moral and spiritual authority, and, most important, they served as role models for Cheyenne children. According to Northern Cheyenne tradition the Council of Chiefs could consist of up to 44 members, but when it called on Campbell, fewer than 35 chiefs belonged. The council rarely inducted new members; generally, it would do so only once every 10 years. Even then, the chiefs felt it was better to leave a place vacant than to fill it with someone who was unworthy of the responsibility.

Republican Michael Strang, a rancher and stockbroker, opposed Campbell in the 1986 race to represent Colorado's Third Congressional District.

Finally Campbell, deeply moved by their offer, agreed. In the summer of 1985, Ben Nighthorse Campbell, the mixed-blood Cheyenne who had grown up in a world that had encouraged him to deny his Native American heritage, became a chief of the Northern Cheyennes. In the years that followed, Campbell's children would also receive their Indian names from the Northern Cheyenne tribe; his daughter, Shanan, would become Sweet Medicine Woman, and Colin would be named Takes Arrows.

Back in Denver, Campbell started to contemplate the next step in his political career. Despite his success in state government, most political analysts insisted that he could never make it in national politics. Campbell was considered too brazen, too outspoken, and too much of a maverick. The people in his small rural district in southwestern Colorado might find that sort of behavior acceptable, but other voters in the state, the critics predicted, would not.

Campbell ignored them. When he announced his intention to run for Congress, he knew he was seeking to represent a voting district with a population of more than half a million people—a group many times larger than the tiny constituency of Colorado's 59th Precinct. His opponent, Republican Michael Strang, a Princeton-educated stockbroker, was heavily favored to retain his seat in the U.S. House of Representatives. Ronald Reagan was in the middle of his second term as president and extremely popular at the time; his popularity with the voters was expected to help Strang and other incumbent Republicans. In fact, it is only rarely that any incumbent member of Congress is defeated; in 1986 only a handful of them lost their bids to return to office.

The election was close, but Campbell upset Strang in a tight finish. When he was sworn into office in January 1987 he became the eighth Native American to have served in the U.S. House of Representatives, out of the many thousands of members in that body's history. In 1988 and 1990 Campbell was reelected to Congress by landslides; in both elections he received about three-quarters of the total vote. The man who had once appeared to be unelectable was beginning to look unbeatable.

6

A PROMISE KEPT

Arriving at the capital in January 1987, Campbell lost no time in making clear to Congress and the rest of the political establishment that he would be doing things his own way. When he learned that the House had a dress code demanding that all of its male members wear traditional suits and ties, Campbell—whose trademark style of dress included a neckerchief and boots—petitioned to have the rules revised. A short time after he entered the U.S. House of Representatives, he persuaded that huge and notoriously slow political body—an assembly of 435 members—to change its code; Congressman Campbell, his colleagues agreed, should be allowed to dress in a manner befitting his own tastes and heritage. Campbell's victory over the forces of conformity delighted those who identified with his rebellious spirit and rural western ways.

Although personally popular among members of both parties, from his first few days in Congress Campbell was not seen as a "team player" by the Democratic party's leaders. Early in his first term he became affiliated with the Conservative Democratic Caucus, a group of about 40 legislators, mainly from southern and western states. That unusual group, which often controlled the balance of power in close contests between the two major parties, was courted by the Republicans and alternately disdained and embraced by other Democrats. Campbell was glad to find Democratic colleagues who supported many of his views, but he would not be constrained by a conservative platform any more than by the Democratic party. Campbell often described himself as a fiscal conservative and a social liberal. Like most conservatives, he emphasized personal responsibility and hard work; he also favored a wide variety of individual rights, an inclination that suspended him between the Democratic and Republican camps.

During his six years in the House of Representatives Campbell served on the House committees on agriculture, the interior, and insular affairs. On environmental matters he continued to vote with the Republicans. One of his causes was a water project that the government had promised the residents of the Southern Ute Indian Reservation. Environmentalists opposed the project; Campbell, complaining of "trust-fund babies who come out to hike in thousand-dollar equipment," urged the government to honor its treaty with the Utes. Later Campbell defended an 1872 act that allowed mining companies to dig for minerals on federal property. He also opposed an increase in grazing fees for ranchers using public lands. Campbell once pointed out that he had never known an environmentalist who was in favor of oil wells, coal mines, or dams. And it was just such works that kept the people in his Colorado district—many of them working-class minorities—employed.

Another issue that divided Campbell from most members of the Democratic party was his position on gun control. As he told one interviewer, one of the first things that he did when he moved to Colorado in 1977 was to ask the local sheriff to deputize him. "I did it so I could carry a gun," he explained. "I was going to jewelry shows almost every week and carrying thousands of dollars worth of merchandise with me, and I wanted to be able to protect my property."

Campbell felt safer carrying a weapon; he also liked guns. He kept six or seven handguns at home in Colorado, and he seldom traveled far from his ranch without carrying at least one of them; he would often tuck another small revolver into his boot for good measure. When he went to Washington, however, he left his guns behind. In the capital he was not licensed even to possess a weapon, let alone carry one. On more than one occasion Campbell wished the Washington laws were different.

In 1991, Washington, D.C., had the highest homicide rate of any major city in the nation. It was in that year that Campbell, well into his third term in Congress, came face-to-face with the capital's crime problem. Campbell was within shouting distance of major government office buildings and on his way to a store near Capitol Hill one evening when he was approached by a man in a dark coat. Demanding the congressman's money, the mugger said he was carrying a gun and would use it if Campbell did not comply. Not one to shy away from life's challenges, and not particularly eager to part with his wallet, Campbell replied, "Oh, yeah? You've got a gun, do you? Let's see it!"

To the mugger it must have looked like an easy contest. In his late fifties, dressed in casual business clothes, and wearing a ponytail, Campbell hardly came across as a tough contender. The mugger, whose bluff had been called, lunged forward, apparently hoping to grab the wallet and run. Campbell seized his attacker and slammed

him to the ground. As the congressman reached down to hold him for the police, the man staggered to his feet and, recalled Campbell, "ran like hell" down the street. Campbell followed him for a few blocks, then gave up.

Campbell reported the incident to the police and met with detectives a few days later. They told him they knew of 62 muggers who "worked" the area where he was attacked. Campbell carefully examined the 62 photographs and picked out six suspects. When the police tried to track them down for a lineup they discovered that

A 1987 photograph offers a panoramic view of the U.S. House of Representatives. Campbell, at this point still wearing a conventional suit and tie, is seated in the fourth row of the semicircle, on the far side of the second aisle.

three of the six were already dead. None of the remaining three turned out to be the culprit.

Campbell refused to give up. He wanted to find the man who had tried to rob him, and he kept looking for him whenever he walked the streets of the neighborhood. Campbell's wife, Linda, disapproved strongly. "Why didn't you just give him the money, Ben?" she would ask. "It's not worth getting killed for!"

Twice Campbell was sure he had spotted the mugger. The first time he immediately hailed a police car, and he and the driver combed the streets of Washington looking for the man, but without success. The second time, he chased the suspect down an alley, losing him after a few hundred feet. Not to be dissuaded, Campbell would continue to look for his assailant as long as he remained in office. If he had been carrying a gun that day, Campbell told his friends, he would have had his man.

Campbell did not object to all gun control laws; the National Rifle Association opposed him the first time he ran for Congress because he supported laws that would ban or strictly regulate metal-jacketed bullets and machine guns. "You don't hunt with metal-jacketed bullets," he later explained. "You use them to kill police officers. And nobody needs a machine gun." Campbell also supported proposals that would require gun sales to include a waiting period between the time a customer requested a gun and the time when he or she could buy it. But apart from these concessions, Campbell, who enjoyed his guns, thought that other people should be allowed to do the same. In his words, "Gun control burns us westerners up!" As Campbell made his convictions clear, the NRA came around; soon the organization was supporting him wholeheartedly.

Campbell's straightforward language and unpretentious style had a great appeal to the voters of Colorado and to many others in the western states. In the late 1980s regional differences played an important role in American politics. On such issues as the environment and gun control, the dividing line fell not so much between parties as between easterners and westerners, between urban dwellers and residents of suburban and rural America. Campbell's district, on the Rocky Mountains' western slope, was to a large extent a region of ranchers, miners, and loggers, and their views on land use and individual rights were very much defined by their livelihoods.

Campbell often felt that he bore a responsibility not only to his district but to citizens all over the rural West; he also felt that he needed to speak for Native Americans. Well aware that he was the only Indian in Congress, Campbell tried his best to represent the interests of the various tribes in his home state, in Montana—his spiritual home, and across the nation. As he put it, "Most members of Congress represent only their own districts, but I have a national constituency."

In addition to his efforts on behalf of the Southern Utes, in 1992 Campbell urged Congress to fund a program to educate residents of Indian reservations on the dangers of drinking during pregnancy. Studies of fetal alcohol syndrome, a form of mental retardation affecting children whose mothers drink heavily while pregnant, showed that 1 in 99 Indian children—six times the percentage in the general population—suffered from the condition. Campbell also argued in favor of legalizing the use of peyote—a psychoactive drug that a number of western tribes had incorporated into their religious rituals—by the Native American Church. Campbell visited reservations when he could, taking note of the needs of various tribes and speaking on such subjects as health and education.

In general, Campbell preferred not to get involved in

intertribal disputes or other disagreements within the Indian community. He did have strong opinions about the antiwhite attitude that he saw at work in some Indian political groups. "The extreme part of the American Indian Movement is as bad as the Ku Klux Klan," he once said. "They don't do Indians any good—they put us back." Campbell also took a firm stand on a controversy that arose in Denver in 1992. That year, the centennial of the Italian explorer Christopher Columbus's arrival in the New World, one Indian group decided to boycott the city's Columbus Day parade. Arguing that Columbus had done little more than bring on the annihilation of the Indian nations, one band of protesters defaced a statue of the explorer. The group called on Campbell to join their boycott. Campbell refused. He later told an interviewer:

Several months after taking office, Campbell looks on as workmen remove an 1868 painting from the House Interior Committee room at the Capitol. The work depicts the scalping of a white man by an Indian, and Campbell, a member of the committee, had argued that the picture was offensive.

I told them they were wrong to deface that statue, and I also told them that I took an oath of office to protect the Bill of Rights. That means that people have a right to hold their parades and express themselves whether you agree with them or not, and I let them know that I would honor the oath I took. It isn't easy being the only Indian in Congress. I've always said that we either need more Indians or no Indians.

The following December, Campbell—dressed in full tribal regalia—rode his horse War Bonnet at the head of the Tournament of Roses parade in Pasadena, California, sharing the title of Grand Marshall with Cristobal Colon, a descendant of Columbus.

Campbell felt that it was better to claim a place in the history and culture of the nation—to let one's presence be felt—than to withdraw from it. It was in this conviction that, early in his congressional career, he set to work on a project that would take him to the end of his third term in the House of Representatives. Campbell had not forgotten how he and and hundreds of other Native Americans had been treated that day in 1976 when they went to the battlefield at the Little Bighorn to honor their fallen ancestors. He could not undo what had happened, but as a U.S. legislator he saw that there was room for change.

Campbell had always found it strange that the site of the battle, which Congress had since designated a national monument, was named the Custer Battlefield. As he recalled in a 1993 interview:

It was the first occasion in history that I've ever heard of where a battlefield was named after the loser. In fact, the policy of the United States, especially concerning battlefields from the Civil War, has been to name these monuments after locations, such as Appomattox Court House or Antietam, rather than for the individuals who fought there.

Dressed in full Cheyenne regalia, Campbell rides his horse War Bonnet in the 103rd Tournament of Roses parade in Pasadena, California, in 1992. To the disapproval of some Indian activists, he shared the role of grand marshal with a descendant of Christopher Columbus.

Not only had Custer lost the battle, but by this time most scholars were refuting what claims he might have held to historical distinction. During his life, Custer had enjoyed a reputation for bravery, but also for irascibility and imprudence. He apparently treated his troops so badly

Native Americans gather to celebrate the renaming of the Custer Battlefield. In the background are the park's visitors center and Last Stand Hill, where the Seventh Cavalry monument and tombstones mark the graves of U.S. soldiers.

that they often deserted, and in 1867 he was court-martialed for his behavior. Before the Little Bighorn, Custer had led the Seventh Cavalry in a series of ruthless and unjustified attacks against the Southern Cheyennes and other tribes in Kansas and on the southern plains. And when he directed his men into battle in 1876, he did so against the orders of his superior officer, guided, by all appearances, only by his own ambition.

Campbell had no desire to glorify the Indians who had won the Battle of the Little Bighorn, but neither did he see a reason why the national monument should honor only Custer, a man whose gifts as a leader were in any case dubious. In order to give visitors a more balanced view of the site's history, the congressman thought the government should erect an additional monument, acknowledging the Indians who fell during the battle, and change the name of the site to the Little Bighorn Battlefield. During his first term in office, he introduced a bill that called for these changes.

For the bill to go into effect, it needed majority approval in the House and the Senate and the signature of the nation's president. Campbell found overwhelming support among his colleagues in the House of Representatives, but in the Senate the response was not so warm. Senator Malcolm Wallop of Wyoming accused Campbell of trying to rewrite history. Campbell's reply was adamant: "We didn't have a chance to write history in the first place." For years, a group of Republican senators struggled to defeat the proposal. An heir to the Custer estate threatened to withdraw the family holdings from the battlefield's historical museum if the name of the site was changed. Campbell continued to lobby. Finally, in 1991, his bill became law.

The following year, Campbell led a ceremonial dance to celebrate the christening of the Little Bighorn Battlefield National Monument. In concrete terms, the victory may have been a small one, but for Campbell and many other Native Americans—people who had long been made to feel like outsiders in their own country—it meant a lot. Campbell explained to a reporter at the site, "Now I feel I am welcome here."

7

A QUESTION OF CHARACTER

When Ben Campbell took a stand on a political issue, he often felt he was speaking on behalf of a certain—usually rural—segment of the American population: ranchers, miners, migrant farm workers, or Native Americans. The congressman sympathized with these groups, he shared their interests, and he wanted to make sure that their views were heard as the government made its decisions. On some questions, however, Campbell claimed no such allegiance; when he took sides on these matters he was acting, he said, purely on his own personal convictions.

One of the most emotionally charged issues that faced the country during Campbell's career in the House was the debate on abortion rights. In the landmark case *Roe v. Wade* in 1973, the Supreme Court had upheld the right of American women to seek abortion in the first three months of pregancy. The ruling allowed for abortion in the second trimester with some restrictions, and in the last trimester if necessary to protect the life of the mother.

Having weathered a bitter campaign, U.S. senator-elect Ben Nighthorse Campbell visits with Democrat Carol Moseley-Braun, the first African-American woman to be elected to the U.S. Senate.

81

Ever since that decision was made, antiabortion groups had been fighting to get it overturned. In the 1980s, under Republican president Ronald Reagan, the antiabortion movement had grown stronger, and when a number of states sought to introduce laws restricting abortion rights, the Supreme Court had to determine whether the *Roe v. Wade* decision would stand.

During the controversy, Campbell disappointed some of his conservative colleagues by arguing consistently and forcefully in favor of abortion rights. Campbell believed that a woman should be free to choose to have an abortion without government restrictions. He had formed his opinion, he said, not on the basis of any particular philosophy or legal argument but on what he had experienced in life. As a deputy sheriff in Sacramento County, he had seen that a young girl faced with a pregnancy would sometimes take her own life to avoid facing her family and society as an unwed mother. Though Campbell did not advocate abortion, as a legislator he was strongly prochoice.

Campbell was just as independent in his positions on defense. When he ran for office in 1986 he joined other Democrats in opposing many of the military's most costly projects. Campbell argued against "Star Wars," the Strategic Defense Initiative, a large-scale, high-technology program championed by Reagan as a means of offsetting Soviet military power. He also opposed the construction of the MX missile, a controversial weapon that Reagan hoped could be added to the nation's defensive arsenal. On top of its preoccupation with the Soviet Union, the U.S. military was at the time deeply involved in the political conflicts of a number of Latin American countries. Campbell opposed the delivery of aid to the Nicaraguan contras, a political and military group fighting to depose that country's leftist government.

Congressman Campbell speaks at a May 1992 celebration honoring land preservation in Colorado.

In 1990, however, as Campbell was reaching the end of his second term in the House, his views on defense took a different turn. That year, when the Iraqi army invaded Kuwait and President George Bush asked Congress to approve his proposal to send U.S. troops to the Middle East, Campbell's conscience led him to support the president. As a Korean War veteran, Campbell knew firsthand the terrible cost of war. When voters called in to express their views, an overwhelming number opposed military involvement in Kuwait. But the congressman did not waver. "We had 1,920 calls against sending the troops to Kuwait, and only 50 calls in favor of it," Campbell later recalled. "But you have to do what you think is right; you have to look down into your soul. I really believed that we'd have to fight it now or fight it later, and maybe on American soil ten years from now." Campbell's views were not always popular, but throughout his career in the House his political courage continued to win him respect.

In November 1990, when Campbell had been elected to his third term in the House of Representatives, he decided that he would run for the position one more time, then go back to his jewelry business and his ranch in Colorado. Campbell enjoyed political life, but he missed his free time, his land, and his artwork.

A short time later Campbell found a reason for rethinking his plan. Colorado's popular incumbent senator Tim Wirth, a Democrat, announced that he had become disenchanted with congressional politics and would not seek reelection in 1992. Wirth's decision opened the floodgates of Colorado politics. Because incumbents are traditionally very difficult to beat, an "open seat" in the House or the Senate always draws out more than the usual number of contenders. In such cases, the candidates generally battle fiercely for their respective party

Kurdish refugees from Iraq surround a supply truck as relief workers distribute crates of frozen chicken. During and after the Persian Gulf War, thousands of Iraqi Kurds, facing persecution in their own country, fled to neighboring lands. Campbell and other advocates of U.S. involvement in the war believed that Iraq's power needed to be checked before it could harm even larger segments of the population.

nominations; the fight between the Democratic and Republican nominees is even harder. Like many other Colorado politicians, Campbell knew that Wirth's decision represented a special, if risky, opportunity.

Before long, former Colorado governor Richard D. Lamm had declared his candidacy for nomination as the Democrats' standard-bearer. Lamm, who in private life had worked as an attorney and a certified public accountant, was one of the most popular elected officials in Colorado history. He had served as governor for three consecutive four-year terms, longer than anyone else before him. During his 12 years in office, a number of his associates had encouraged him to seek the presidency.

Once Lamm entered the race, many political analysts assumed it was over. The primary election, they thought,

Campbell talks with Colorado ranchers before the start of a debate between the congressman and Democratic opponents Richard Lamm and Josie Heath. Ranchers and other representatives of the rural West were among Campbell's most consistent allies.

would be a mere formality. Campbell's people disagreed. And Campbell himself, although his intention to retire from politics had been sincere, soon came around to their point of view. He knew the race would be difficult, but he may have felt that if he was going to leave office it would be better to go out with a bang, seeking an unlikely six-year term in the U.S. Senate, than to retire quietly after another two years in the House of Representatives.

Campbell's race against Lamm contained a certain irony; in 1986 it had been Lamm who first encouraged Campbell to run for a seat in Congress. The governor could not have known that he was helping to bring about his own defeat—and perhaps the end of his political career—only six years later. On August 11, 1992, the unlikely occurred, and Ben Nighthorse Campbell won the Democratic party nomination for the U.S. Senate. Campbell received 117,634 votes to Lamm's 93,599. Josie Heath, the other leading candidate, placed a distant third with 47,418 votes.

Campbell's victory had been decisive, but it was no landslide. He had garnered the nomination with about 45 percent of the vote. It had been a difficult battle, and now he had to face the Republicans' wealthy and well-rested candidate, Terry Considine. Campbell's primary race had been relatively free of ill feelings among the candidates. Lamm and Campbell respected each other, and the former governor had accepted his defeat with grace. The general election would be different; it would be bitter, vicious, and unpredictable.

The race between Campbell and Considine was in a way a contest between two different worlds. A comparison of the candidates' histories made them look like extreme versions of the Republican and Democratic prototypes. When Campbell, a high school dropout from a poor family in California, was on his way to the Korean War

in 1951, Considine, another Californian, 14 years younger, was growing up on his family's ranch in the San Diego foothills. When Campbell was living in Tokyo, training for the 1964 Olympics, Considine was attending the

Campbell accepts congratulations from competitor Josie Heath after receiving the Democratic nomination for the 1986 U.S. Senate race.

Groton School, an expensive eastern preparatory academy. Campbell had gone on to build a life for himself as an educator, law enforcer, and craftsman. Considine had studied at Harvard University. Campbell and Considine were men of vastly different experience, and each would try to turn the distinctive character of his life to his own advantage.

As it turned out, Campbell's working-class background and independent route to leadership worked in his favor. Most voters could identify better with a man who had fought alone for his success than with one who had enjoyed the support of a wealthy and well-connected family. And Considine was, in any case, clearly the less experienced candidate. Before he had ever held a public office Considine had run for the U.S. Senate once, in 1986, and lost. He had been appointed—not elected—to the Colorado Senate the following year to fill a vacant seat, and then had been elected to a second term as an incumbent. Considine had no political background outside the state senate, and he had never won an election as an outsider.

Campbell's campaign emphasized his interest in the situation of working people. While he continued to bill himself as a fiscal conservative—opposing, for example, the capital-gains tax and other taxes that drew profits away from big business—he spoke in favor of government investment in education and job training, and he supported an increase in income tax on the wealthy. Considine, generally considered an archconservative, not only favored the economic policy of the Reagan and Bush administrations but sided with the religious right on social issues. Although environmentalists were reluctant to endorse either candidate, they threw their support to Campbell, who, it was said, would at least listen to the liberal side.

The first opinion polls gave Campbell an enormous lead; some of them showed him ahead of Considine by more than 20 percentage points. When the results came out, the general election was only weeks away. Considine would have to attack swiftly if he wanted a chance against his popular rival.

Campbell, meanwhile, had his own weak points. Among them was his notoriously short—according to one reporter, "ferocious"—temper. Campbell also had an unorthodox way of dealing with journalists whose work he did not approve of. He was not interested, he said, in making life easy for a hostile press. If a reporter said or wrote something he disagreed with, he rebelled. The congressman's hometown newspaper, the *Durango Herald*, had for the most part enjoyed a friendly relationship with him ever since he entered the Colorado legislature in 1982. When Campbell was starting his third term in Congress, however, he began to believe that the *Herald*'s editors had developed a bias against him, and he abruptly broke off all communication with the paper. While Campbell's staff continued to keep all of the other newspapers and media representatives in his voting district informed of his positions and activities, they were told they should "give no interviews, answer no questions, and not respond to any letters or questions if they come from the *Herald*." In a letter to Richard Ballentine, publisher of the *Herald*, Campbell claimed that one of the paper's editors was "out to discredit, humiliate and/or insult me under the guise of [editorial policy]." Campbell's boycott continued for more than 14 months; he and Ballentine only made peace after a *Herald* editorial indicated that Campbell would make an excellent candidate for the U.S. Senate.

Campbell had gotten what he wanted, but his reputation was probably not the better for it. Still, the political climate could not have been worse for Considine; in the presidential elections, the incumbent Bush was struggling desperately to cut into the lead of his Democratic challenger, Bill Clinton. By all appearances, the Republicans were headed for disaster, and they would probably take Considine with them.

Then the press dealt Campbell a bitter blow. A series of articles, most of them appearing in the *Rocky Mountain News,* began to question Campbell's accounts of his early life. Some of them accused him of exaggerating the amount of time he had spent in St. Patrick's Children's Home. Campbell, the articles said, had spoken of living in the orphanage for "several years," when in fact his

Terry Considine, Republican candidate for U.S. Senate, talks with the press during a campaign stop in Durango, Colorado. Campbell's race against Considine took a bitter turn shortly before the election.

stay had been closer to six months. Campbell attributed the discrepancy to a poor memory and to his inability, as a child of two, to measure the passage of time the way adults do. Another article disparaged Campbell for telling a reporter he had been caught behind enemy lines in the Korean War. Campbell denied having made the statement. In themselves, the charges raised against Campbell were fairly trivial, but they were challenging one of the congressman's main sources of appeal—his integrity. The Senate race tightened.

Many of Colorado's leading newspapers endorsed Considine. Some said that, while Campbell portrayed himself as a reformer, he was in fact a tax-and-spend Democrat who had a habit of missing committee meetings. Campbell's publicity crew came back with television spots in which he appeared on horseback, silhouetted against the sunset. It was, as Considine's campaign manager complained, a slick image and an effective one, but it could not fully offset the negative campaign being waged against Campbell. Ten days before election day his lead had shrunk dramatically. It was beginning to look as if the Cheyenne congressman, the man who had never lost an election, might lose his place in history to an obscure state legislator.

By this time, however, Considine was starting to have image problems of his own. Some reporters asserted that his claims of success in business were vastly overblown. Others pointed out that he had been less than forthcoming when asked about his military draft status during the Vietnam War, when he was a student at Harvard. Like Campbell, Considine had lived in many other places before settling in Colorado. The media criticized some of his real estate dealings in other states—particularly a plan to make condominiums out of a housing complex in Atlanta, Georgia, which might have displaced the complex's elderly residents. In the end, the charges Considine faced were more serious than the claims that had been leveled at Campbell.

Finally, in November 1992, the people of Colorado made their decision. Considine finished a respectable second, receiving 655,236 votes to Campbell's 796,472. A heavy crossover vote by Republicans and a good showing on the part of independent voters had assured Campbell's victory.

In January 1993, at the age of 59, Ben Nighthorse Campbell—farmhand, athlete, teacher, artist, rancher, police officer, and Cheyenne chief—was sworn into office as a U.S. Senator. It was a career he would be entitled to

U.S. Senate candidate Ben Nighthorse Campbell and his son, Colin, wait for their ballots on election day, November 3, 1992.

Campbell, in his trademark ponytail and western hat, visits Fortunoff, a New York store that sells his jewelry, shortly after his election to the U.S. Senate.

keep for at least six years; beyond that, his future, he knew from experience, might hold anything.

When he was interviewed shortly after he reached his seat in the Senate, Campbell offered his own thoughts on what lay ahead. He predicted that Clinton would seek reelection in 1996, and that he would win. He expected to support Vice-President Albert Gore in the two presidential elections to follow. Campbell mused:

> When Al Gore is through at the White House, I'll be 75 years old, and I think that's too old to run for the presidency—probably. . . . I might just run for governor of Colorado someday. I think it would be poetic justice for a Cheyenne to lead the state where the Sand Creek massacre occurred. And I wouldn't rule out becoming Secretary of the Interior, if it were ever offered to me.

Of all his many identities, the senator knew there was at least one he had yet to explore. "After I was elected to the Senate," he explained, "I got a letter from the president of Portugal, who said that I was the only Portuguese-American ever to serve in the U.S. Senate. You know, I might like to be Ambassador to Portugal someday."

CHRONOLOGY

1933   Born on April 13 in Auburn, California

1950   Quits high school at age 17, travels throughout American West

1951   Enlists in U.S. Air Force; joins air police unit in Korea

1953   Honorably discharged from air force

1958   Awarded bachelor of arts degree in fine arts and physical education from San Jose State University

1960   Moves to Japan to study judo

1963   Wins gold medal in judo at Pan-American Games in São Paulo, Brazil

1964   Enters Tokyo Olympics as captain of the U.S. judo team

1966   Marries Linda Price, one of his judo students

1972   Recruited by Sacramento County Sheriff's Department; serves as deputy sheriff until 1977

1976   Becomes a member of Northern Cheyenne tribe; Cheyenne leaders give him the name *Nighthorse* in memory of his great-grandfather, Black Horse, who fought Custer in the Battle of the Little Bighorn

1977   Moves to southwestern Colorado with wife and children; begins ranching and raising quarter horses; wins acclaim as Indian jewelry maker

1982   Wins upset victory against Republican opponent and is elected to Colorado House of Representatives

1986   Elected to U.S. House of Representatives; will be reelected to the House by a landslide in 1988 and again in 1990

1992   Persuades Congress to rename the Custer Battlefield the Little Bighorn Battlefield and to add a monument to the site in honor of the Indians who died there; elected to U.S. Senate

FURTHER READING

Ambrose, Stephen E. *Crazy Horse and Custer.* New York: Meridian/Penguin, 1975.

Brown, Dee. *Bury My Heart at Wounded Knee.* New York: Henry Holt, 1991.

Catlin, George. *North American Indians.* New York: Penguin, 1989.

Davies, Philip J., and Fredric A. Waldstein, eds. *Political Issues in America Today.* New York: St. Martin's Press, 1988.

Fromm, Alan, and Nicolas Soames. *Judo: The Gentle Way.* New York: Routledge, Chapman & Hall, 1982.

Hoig, Stan. *The Cheyenne.* New York: Chelsea House, 1989.

Josephy, Alvin M., Jr. *Red Power: The American Indians' Fight for Freedom.* Lincoln: University of Nebraska Press, 1985.

Loomis, Burdett. *The New American Politician: Elected Entrepreneurs and the Changing Style of Political Life.* New York: Basic Books, 1988.

Mails, Thomas E. *Dog Soldiers, Bear Men and Buffalo Women.* Englewood Cliffs, NJ: Prentice-Hall, 1973.

Sandoz, Mari. *Cheyenne Autumn.* Lincoln: University of Nebraska Press, 1953.

INDEX

PICTURE CREDITS

CHRISTOPHER HENRY is a New York attorney specializing in American immigration law. He is the author of two books on U.S. immigration law, a biography of the civil rights leader Julian Bond, and a biography of Chief Justice William H. Rehnquist, which will be included in the Chelsea House series THE JUSTICES OF THE UNITED STATES SUPREME COURT. Since 1990, he has been an accredited delegate to the United Nations, where he represents the Brehon Law Society, an association of attorneys and jurists concerned with human rights and the administration of justice in Northern Ireland.

W. DAVID BAIRD is the Howard A. White Professor of History at Pepperdine University in Malibu, California. He holds a Ph.D. from the University of Oklahoma and was formerly on the faculty of history at the University of Arkansas, Fayetteville, and Oklahoma State University. He has served as president of both the Western History Association, a professional organization, and Phi Alpha Theta, the international honor society for students of history. Dr. Baird is also the author of *The Quapaw Indians: A History of the Downstream People* and *Peter Pitchlynn: Chief of the Choctaws* and the editor of *A Creek Warrior of the Confederacy: The Autobiography of Chief G. W. Grayson.*